Poems from the Battlefield

Katherine Mercurio Gotthardt

Copyright © 2009 Katherine Mercurio Gotthardt
All rights reserved.

www.PoemsfromtheBattlefield.com

ISBN: 1-4392-5448-6
ISBN-13: 9781439254486

Dedication

For David, who has lived my battle with me, and who has been my husband, healer, friend and beloved.

Table of Contents

Part I: The Brief Present
The Second Civil War 2
Guided Tour 3
View from Behind the Hill 4
Meeting the Regiment 5
To the Hikers 7
Poem from the Battlefield 8

Part II: The Long, Supposed Past
Enlisting 12
The Luncheon Ladies 13
Spectator Sport 15
Battlefield Haiku 17
War Preferred 18
Standpoint 19
Blue Child 20
The Red Flagged House 23
Speaking to Specters 25
It Might be a Mountain 27
The Spoils 29
Delayed Reaction 31
Assault Weapon 32
Canteen 33
I am at War with my Body 35

Casualties of War	36
Crossing the Line	38
The Sergeant's Words	40
Stonewall Down	41
Maneuvers	42
Commander-in-Chief	43
Chinn Ridge Ruins	44
Untitled	45
For the Red Badge	46
Resuming	48
Winter's Prisoner	49
After the Armies	50
The Prison Camp Survivors	52
Endurance Test	53
I Prefer to Remember	55
Battle Hymn	56
Afterword	57

Part I:
The Brief Present

"We must not be enemies." -Abe Lincoln

"I found we were fighting that great battle over again..."
 -Captain Henry T. Owen, C

The Second Civil War
for J. P. M.

While we failed to give it attention,
we were captured by the tension

stalking the unwary:
the debates, the issues, the parry,

the throttling, ignorant arrogance,
the slow closing fist of intolerance,

the partisan struggle for dominance,
and the murder of compassion and competence.

"...Our losses during the two days' battle in killed, wounded, and missing, according to the official lists sent in, are 92 officers and 1,891 noncommissioned officers and privates.."
                                    -*Major Gen. Franz Sigel*

Guided Tour
Behind the Stone Bridge

No one to lead you
but a dirty map.

Follow their faces.
Ask them, why do

cracked trees bend
but still leak sap?

When did these woods
stop brandishing boys?

How did they teach
these children to hide,

to shoot at every noise?
Turn your eyes to the creek,

and then again to the guide.
If you run, be quick.

Or you will part the forest
as if you were the dawn.

View from Behind the Hill
Manassas, 2005

From here, the view up on the hill is blind;
across the street dissolves in hectic days
as every driver inching through the line
obstructs the passage back across that way.

Travelers trapped in traffic frown, distraught—
the cell connections here are always dead,
and as you crawl in transit, speeding thoughts
race me to the highway in your stead.

Roads rise like mountains, monuments still stand;
sepulchers, relentless, grimace gray. You've
been grounded like a ship condemned to land,
your stillness painful as I start to move.

You sit cemented, and of course, I'm torn
you barely idle while I am transformed.

Meeting the Regiment

Four miles of no one
but deer—no wonder sudden
sounds of their voices

startle me. I slip on ancient
shades, and when I look up
they are there—

not one, but fifty or so,
soldiers, wool jackets,
a gray regiment

re-enacting war,
marching the furious routes
of old convictions,

standing stark in cool,
April air against the hay.
Shocked at first, I half

smile, seeing myself from
their eyes: modern woman,
Yankee, trusting fate

to Confederates.
They stand straight at
attention, tip their broad hats,

nod, Good Morning, Ma'am,
men lowering chivalrous eyes
as I slowly pass.

To the Hikers

Your spring stroking of
young grass on bare feet
insults petrified monuments

to those torn-booted boys,
the ones with bruised
aching arches and streams
from wounded toes.

Grass turns caustic,
not erotic silliness
for urban hikers.

Are you resentful
I've intruded, ruined your
weekend getaway?

This is no field for love.
We call it sacred ground.
Put your shoes back on.

Pick up your backpack.
Feed your sandwich to the
crows. March to early death.

Poem from the Battlefield

Soft stepping fall leaves
settle on these battle trails,
quiet march of ghosts.

My mother believed
my soul is damned, for I fail
to take wine and host.

Mother need not grieve—
though we know all soldiers flail
at enemy boasts,

and troops die in sheaves,
these acres still help to hail
ideals. I come close

to the white birch trees
saluting through still-green vale,
my god's command post.

Mother, be relieved.
Here, full life and death prevail.
I AM saved—almost.

Part II:
The Long, Supposed Past

"Well, well, General, bury these poor men
and say no more of it."

-Robert E. Lee

Enlisting

**Here is a list of what I
want to do before I die:**

**to love without reserve; to peel apart
the wool that serves to bind and blind my heart;
to feel for once without thought, let the hot
blood of holy human nature release
control; to stand before the line,
opening arms, inviting certain death, resign
to taking beautiful breath
and live.**

Did you ever have a list?

"We could not conceive it could happen,
so madness defeated our doubt,
pummeled by palpability,
disbelief cowering in corners
ill-suited for anyone's safety."

The Luncheon Ladies
for M.A.S.

**An acre or two of parasols
and lace, broods**

**of sliced cucumber and bread,
sweet berry desserts,**

**nests of silk fans made the
play-perfect gander**

**for flocks. Pluming themselves
for imminent victory**

**in this show of a gentleman's
war, chirping antebellum
anthems in heated secessionist
sun, the applause**

**for the sharp-looking soldiers
approaching, white hands**

**cracked at the air,
the deafening splinter of gunshot…**

What did they think of
just then?

Did refined smiles flee
from their faces,

frantic hordes driven off?
Did they drop

strawberry tarts to hurtle and help
or did they just sit there

in shock? In time, they must have
gone home again.

But, what
did they say to their children?

"A time comes when silence is betrayal."
  -Rev. Dr. Martin Luther King, Jr.

Spectator Sport

There were those who thrived on war, beasts slaking life from the whiff of an army, the lusty challenge of pulverizing people, mutilating sweaty, opposing ideals that spurred them into ire. For months, we spied on their perilous

padding across our fields crushed flat, tracts of mud collecting between their claws, tails and anger dragged behind. We sat silent, watched them furrow ferocity, swallow and store it deep in sloshing bellies, testicles slapping sides of their thighs, grinning growl of certain attack, the fanged wonton

of animals. And we in our holes and hovels and homes peeked through our filthy curtains, hid behind dry rotting boards, winced at the warning rumble we knew would lead only to death. We crouched beneath sills and sounds, sniffed the air for scorching, secretly scanned the land, submerged in foray—but safe.

Our silence shrieked louder than the victims that followed, the spill of body and heart and artillery on our neat fences and farms, the kind of dying we believed would only happen in hell. We bit our tongues and we waited, drawing blood from our only hope, sucking it in, and down, back into ourselves, hiding it in the crawlspaces of our hearts, so when later we

remembered, we could do nothing more than descend to the floor, force our foreheads into hot hands, rub our eyes blind in our palms, try to outscream whispers that would not abandon our ears, draw our patched knees to our shoulders, and rock to the rhythm of shame.

"The battle is over, and although we did not succeed in pushing the enemy out of their strong position, I am sure they have not any thing to boast about. They have lost at least as many in killed and wounded as we have. We have taken more prisoners from them than they have from us."
— *Private Louis Leon*

Battlefield Haiku

He said it was about pride,
some kind of principles.

I see dead people.

War Preferred
apologies to Langston Hughes

What happens to war preferred?

Does it pile up
like steaming mounds of dung?

Or pierce like buckshot
through skin, to bone, to lung?

Does it dress itself in values, truth or need?
Or does it stand alone
and bleed?

Maybe it just devours
our every sense of self.

Or will it kill itself?

Standpoint

Three lifetimes back
when I was gay and black
and I wore a gray uniform like you
did, and I shot the same bullets you
did, and I watched love bleed as yours
did—did you think I didn't grieve as you
did, because I was gay and black?

Blue Child

Never had it occurred to me
your tears would look like mine,
here, your thin, body bent across my porch,

face a pot burnt in the fire,
agitated by flame, blaze
striking out and up to squelch each drop

wetly disrupting its burn. No, I
did not think I would meet at my door
North soldier, dark soldier,

tired as resigning day, that I'd recognize
that sinful sadness, the one that has eaten
our good years gone, the ever-smolder

of embers and anger, built by coal
and smoke and iron and labor,
raked daily of expendable ashes,

making room for another night's
meal. I did not know I would see you,
my younger, freer self, that I would ever

look in your expiring eyes, the eyes
I should see as my enemy's,

that all I would see is a crying child,
wearing the burden of blue.

"Help one another is part of the religion of our sisterhood." *-Louisa May Alcott*

The Red Flagged House

You say you are here to protect us,
the man-less, the son-less, the tepid wives
wafting through misused rooms of our
home-turned-makeshift-hospital. But
the divan is upholstered in wounded,

dun rags stacked on our armoire,
gauze, iodine, ammonia, spirits following
the hems of our dresses. "We cannot fit
one more!" we cry. But you are deaf with war.
"We have nothing left to give you!" we

wail, but the moans of our warriors bury us
in bandages and heat rash and fungus. Our dresser
lies on its back, an oaken cot for Confederates,
our maple table forced to feed soldiers to surgeons,
and everywhere, blood of our bold and our young

re-paints our wood, our walls, our memories.
We shuttle torn uniforms from what was home
to hearth, stir some in our soup cauldrons, burn others
to stay the fire, the fetid smoke of our torched ideals and
stained coverlets greeting each new casualty.

You say you are here to protect us, we your women
who don't want war, we who try to heal hurts,
scouring basins with our old lace, sucking up sweat
with our linens, mending the last blankets we own,
and asking, "Who will protect us from you?"

"We built fires all over the battle field and the dead of the blue and gray were being buried all night, and the wounded carried to the hospital."
                    -*Corporal Horatio D. Chapman*

Speaking to Specters

**Through your ageless eyes,
I understand your replies
to what you most fear:**

**trembling from the tip
of the fuse to the cannon's
opening, the rip**

**in the air of civil
war, tear in the veil that lies:**
'there is but one truth.'

**You can never know
for sure where the dying go,
leaving us the rot.**

Only those mindless
enough not to think are not
distressed at our hot

blood seeping from wounds
to grass, to dirt, to cold stones,
to earth's heart below,

union of bodies
with things we cannot see, and
more we will not know.

It Might be a Mountain

From where we stand,
it might be a mountain
of hay or of hell,
this looming terrain.

We limp in split boots,
torn coats and commands
like starved deer in their
skins in winter, and
we whisper through weeds,
we cough through wet leaves
piling like corpses
beneath ancient trees.

Trudging up hills
and dredging our flasks,
we want water and wishes again.
And we muse on the honor
of protecting the gray,
through hills of briars
and summits of clay.

We soldiers of glory,
some, barely-grown,
beg for our breath
without really knowing
which battles we fight,
what forts we defend,
what is an enemy,
or who is a friend.

The Spoils

You revel in my fear,
pay with humanity for
a feast of terror,
relish the choke of my fingers
with ropes while you thirst,
waiting to see me writhe or hear
me whimper. You know
I will not yield.

I refuse to leak a sound
for your satisfaction, enticing
your taste for challenge,
your arousal swelling
like a starved stomach.

Were I weak and pathetic,
your interest would drop.
But I am not. You thrive
on lengthening

torture, growing your flaccid
ego, each moment adding
to your lust and laughter.
You prefer my fright to my death,
my panic to pain, but I prefer
life despite you. I refuse to die.

But you refuse to free me.
You mark my mind
for your pleasure, my body
as your monument,
my spirit for quiet death,

and you call it
spoils of war.

Delayed Reaction

Even now, I cannot
cast off that
beaten memory,
the one that carries
the belt, the long, dark coat,
the serpentine smirk.

I try to make sense of it, try
to analyze, intellectualize,
but it will not subside,
my unforgiving mind's eye

recalling fatty fingers roping
throat, the pulse of sub-animal
seething, the words no human
should use, the stillness of true

terror, and the deathless wish
that you would be gone.

"Well, it is all over now. The battle is lost, and many of us are prisoners, many are dead, many wounded bleeding and dying. Your Soldier lives and mourns and but for you, my darling, he would rather, a million times rather, be back there with his dead, to sleep for all time in an unknown grave."
-Major Gen. George Pickett

Assault Weapon

**You say, "There is always
someone worse off,"
as if we've no right to pain.**

**Why not just go and
invite the troop back
to assault us again and again?**

Canteen

I have followed you steady wherever you've led,
stuck by your hip and your horse's flank,
held my own for your thirsty need and
given you what you've wanted.

Most days I am barely cool
and others, I am rank with your sweat,
thin rim melted smooth by your sucking,
my own skin already dry.

Some days I am empty and you damn me,
others you soak me to the brim,
pinning me under and making me drink,
force me to hold more than I'm made for.

Still, I want you to live from the liquid in me,
the stuff that will keep you alive,
but you fill me with water from the stream
they have poisoned. If you touch
your lips to me, you could die.

How you survive is a mystery to me,
but who am I to wonder?
My fate is knotted to you,
and you will lose use for me.

There are plenty of others like me,
those who have served their soldiers.
You toss us in victory, drop us in fields,
leave us to be trampled by horses.

Our last ounces of life weep back into earth
as you dance your battalions back home.

I Am at War with My Body

In the darkness of paralyzed dawn,
I am at war with my body.
Fingers and knees creaky as cannon wheels,
thighs and feet headstones
to today's great battle
and whatever may come from the North—

I am at war with my body.
Back and bottom barely covered
by the last bits of a horsehair blanket,
spine a remnant of yesterday's burdens,
stiff as the will of my General,
bruised as the shoulders of mares—

I am at war with my body.
In spiteful morning more dark with my dread
than any barrel I've looked down into,
any soot I've ever swallowed, any eyes
I've ever lied into about the glory of war—

I am at war with my body.
More, my mouth can't move to say.
I am at war with my body.
And so I start the day.

"Character is like a tree, and reputation its shadow. The shadow is what we think it is; the tree is the real thing."
-Abraham Lincoln

Casualties of War

In the conservative shadow of trees
and beyond the camp boundaries,

from behind your own masked
war, I still hear you ask,

"Who do you think I am?"
And I, as carefully as I can,

squint through the settling evening
clouded with fear and what we believe in,

try to examine your uniform, your look—
suppressed, stonewalled, expressionless. I am ab-
scessed,

wounded by thought, needing rest
blinded from trails of endless

gray, from this march, a ceaseless succession
of ignorance, from the fatigue of guessing—

and you, a stranger who asks but will not tell,
fall victim to my private hell:

your question taunts each battle injury,
and I mistake you for my enemy.

"Government cannot endure permanently half slave, half free..."

-Abraham Lincoln

Crossing the Line

Were it not for barbed wire
and thicket and thorn
and mud that stands its own ground,

I might attempt or be tempted
to cross to the field
where the trails are confounded

by opposite minds
and the weapons they wield:
tracks of hoof-prints and rut-rifts

and puddles and holes,
the scent of battalions
that swear they are free.

Were it not for my General,
my brothers, my neighbors,
I might try to unite

these fierce armies in me.

The Sergeant's Words

Wool is an itchy havoc—
I wear balm to soothe my skin,
hives swelling and reddening within
my uniformed self. Between

murky war-torn boundaries,
when fields have emptied themselves
of blood-soaked soldiers and rebels,
I rip the white wool from my back,
inhale the dismembered day,
taste gunpowder setting a trap:

I curse my men and damn them
for failure in this battle-burnt air,
my own cannon fire assaulting them
like an enemy's arrogant dare.

Stonewall Down

You told me to build a wall from rubble,
fragments of earth and strength and clay;
you told me to stack stones, one on another,
fill cracks in with dust and mud.
I did what I was told.

There was no way it would ever hold.

It came crashing down on an exhale.

"He lay the succeeding two days and nights helpless on the field, between the city and those grim terraces of batteries his company and regiment had been compell'd to leave him to his fate."

-Walt Whitman

Maneuvers

I watch your maneuvers,
study close your steps through
grass and bramble, bumble behind
trying not to stumble.

But this pack is heavy,
this uniform hot,
my body laden with unnatural weight.

I place my boot in your print before me,
follow your blue lead,
and pray to God I can trust you.

"I cannot trust a man to control others who cannot control himself."

-Robert E. Lee

Commander-in-Chief

You steer us south
through the pine-tree tunnel,
iced cones incoming
through needles, snow,
and prayers for our dead.
Our feet are bloody.
Our clothes are torn.
We reek from the squelched
fuse of understanding.
We follow you like addiction,
begging for bits of regular rest,
weekly bites of bread,
salvation from this frozen cup,
and respite from the memories
of our dead.

The Chinn Ridge Ruins
A triolet

Heavily booted, persisting through snow,
over soldiers, silenced in death's white womb,

winter rustling where old war stories grow.
Heavily booted, persisting through snow,

grey, childlike specters from long ago,
uniformed visage from premature tombs.

Heavily booted, persisting through snow,
over soldiers, silenced in death's white womb.

Untitled

I peer in the maw of the cannon:

opaque

icy

empty.

Your words come to mind.

For the Red Badge

I march with you but
have no wisdom of deep cut,
or the plains horse rut,

or the ridge at Chinn,
or really anything in
your blue-gray warring.

I'm marching with you,
but my jacket is see-through
and my boots too new.

I would flog myself
if I believed it would help
transcend me to hell,

rid me of this need
to leave, cowardice that feasts
on a better me.

Temptations seduce
me from keeping time with you.
My laces are loose.

I want to conform,
be worthy of uniform,
serve as I have sworn.

Put this down before
I choose that I must die or
help you win this war.

Resuming

There is no thornier victory
than brushes with ancient brambles,
then the gallop back to group

to fall back into line,
to straighten the collar,
to button the coat,
to tuck pants into boots
in time to attend
to the endless,
meaningful march.

Winter's Prisoner

This frozen grass, shattered glass
from some rough blower,
Your careless boots,

the lead of men like you
through the shards of wrecking,
your rifle at my back, your voice
cold as a northern river:
"You have no rights here, Yankee."

When we reach your encampment,
the true test will begin:
every morning's rope-burned wrists,
a smattering of grits,
two sips of black coffee
from your dented cup,

no more until you've marched me miles
through your fields of ice.

"Every creature is better alive than dead, men and moose and pine trees, and he who understands it aright will rather preserve its life than destroy it."
—*Henry David Thoreau*

After the Armies

How do we manage the minutes
we've wished right out of time,
the places we pretend we never have been,
what we've cauterized out of our minds?

How do we manage barracks,
or tents, or guard shacks, or scandal,
or two empty buckets poured into the cracks
dividing the driest of earth? Thorned bush

marks a country torn, plants dense with phony
polemics, we stink of those who say they believe.
We cover our ears with weathered hands
as we scream, "Enough!"

How do we manage this pitiful bit
of logical sun snuffed out? What of assumptions
that kept us alive? Where should we bury
our hearts and our memories

to uncover after the war?

And will we be able to find them again when armies have been there before?

The Prison Camp Survivors

I must have lived on a memory:
there was nothing in that camp
but hiding, confining, despising,
guarded wood that hedged us in,
thick talk of bombastic fear,
bragging that kept us breathing.

I'd stare you down on any day,
hold my thin patch of ground, refuse
to walk away, my stubborn fury feeding
starving resolve, the relentless rush of self
preservation, and the need to protect a nation.

What is it that kept us alive so long
when cages held us fast? Was it hope or will
or stupidity? Competitive pride or vanity?

Or was it the raven circling our minds,
daring *our* dare to survive?

Endurance Test

We used to play a game.
We called it endurance,
kids in a barn on a hot day,
dressed in winter clothes and hay,
windows shut up tight,
sun beating the building like
a fist, swelter building like
a storm. We'd see who
could last longest and who
would want mercy the soonest.
We'd hold our breaths, let
sweat and panic breathe for us,
a competition of pain. Who would
falter first? I always won,

always outstayed the others who
gasped for arid air. I knew how
to inhale hard and hold. I knew how
to hurt and keep quiet. I joined the war

at sixteen, endurance enlisting
with me. Four years of war and more,
I survived the perennial march. I held
the heaviest pack. I could walk
without water, wear the white flannel

and wool of our regiment even in August.
There was nothing I could not
carry like a mercenary. Except
that unseasonable afternoon,
the General held his hat to heart,
for the first time, seeing our eyes, his own
muggy with the graying day, he told us
the war was over. He told us
we could all go home. He told us
all to live our lives, to find
our mothers, our sisters, our children

our wives. And I remember thinking,
what home? What life? What family
and what wife? I was made for endurance.
What would I do without war?

I Prefer to Remember

I prefer to remember
that morning,

the sun burnishing trees,
wreath of light
about your head,

your face a Christmas
I had not seen
since before we went to war.

Battle Hymn
for David

When the world has all forgotten
why it went to war,
and when the cannons cease
to pummel anymore,
I will return to you
no matter my condition
and sing our hymn of victory
in personal rendition:

Tears and swords and sweat, my love,
haven't scarred my mind so deeply
that I won't trample through these thorns
to loose my love completely.

Afterword

Though the context is historical, Poems from the Battlefield is an exceedingly present, personal collection operating on several levels-the literal, the sociological, the psychological and the metaphorical. The poems are not strictly factual. I am not a historian, and I leave interpretive details to the talented professionals in that field.

These poems are, in part, my attempts to reconcile the incongruity between defending values and deliberately killing neighbors and loved ones. By using persona, I thrust myself into characters, soldiers, prisoners, civilians, families, friends-because that is the only way I know how truly to connect with history.

And even after having written these poems, I cannot fathom how we could have allowed ourselves to war with one another.

Most of my context and photos come from

Manassas Battlefield Park, Manassas Museum, Bristoe Station and Brentsville Courthouse Historic
Center. The obviously older photos come from the National Archives and Library of Congress. The quotes come from a variety of open, online sources and archives.

In some poems, you might recognize relationships between past and present historic struggles with our current domestic climate of fear that prevents us from being our best selves.

And you will see violence and anger and torture, because those are what war is about. These were the themes most difficult for me to express, because these also represent my personal battles with violence, rape, PTSD, manipulation, harassment, inadequate mental healthcare and major depression. Though the incidents all occurred within 6-7 months in 2005, the effects remain. But poetry is a healing art, and my trials have been petty compared to the years of pain that our civil conflict caused, and indeed, that all warring causes.

There were many times I thought of abandoning this project. Too personal, I thought. Too poorly written. Too liable to bring up history I do not wish to recall.

But there is a difference between recalling and re-living.

We must always recall. We must never re-live.

-Katherine Mercurio Gotthardt